D1402390

TOP 10 QUARTERBACKS

BY K. C. KELLEY

Published by The Child's World®
1980 Lookout Drive • Mankato, MN 56003-1705
800-599-READ • www.childsworld.com

Photo credits:
AP Photo: 14, 15. Joe Robbins: 4, 5, 6, 7, 8, 9, 10, 11,
12, 13, 16, 19. Adobe Stock: abhbah05 21. Shutter-
stock: EKFS Cover, 2; Carlos E. Santa Maria (cover,
1), Goir 4 (hand).

ISBN: 9781503827202
LCCN: 2017960460

Printed in the United States of America
PA02380

CONTENTS

WHO'S NUMBER ONE?

At the end of a football game, everyone knows who won. It's the team with the most points! At the end of the NFL season, the No. 1 team is clear. It's the winner of the Super Bowl. Choosing the No. 1 **quarterback** of all time is a bit harder. Is it the player with the most Super Bowl rings? Or the player with the most **touchdown** passes? Is it the passer with the highest rating? Or the one who played in the most games? Fans, experts, and fellow players all have their opinions.

Opinions are different than facts. Facts are real things. Joe Montana won four Super Bowls. That's a fact. Joe Montana is handsome. That's an **opinion**. A football field is 100 yards long. That's a fact. Lambeau Field is the best place to watch a football game. That's an opinion.

Joe
Montana

WE'RE
#1

Some people might think Montana is not handsome. That's fine; that's their opinion. But they can't say he didn't win four Super Bowls. That's a fact. Packers fans think Lambeau is No. 1. But you would find a very different opinion in lots of other NFL stadiums, where fans think THEIR place is No. 1.

And that's where *you* come in. You get to choose who is the greatest quarterback in NFL history. You will read lots of facts and stories about these great players. Based on those, what's your opinion? There are no wrong answers about who is the greatest quarterback of all time . . . but you might have some fun discussions with your football-loving pals!

Read on and then after you're done, make up your own Top 10 list (for more details, see page 20).

Peyton Manning

NUMBERS, NUMBERS	
All-Time Career Passer Rating (through 2017)	
1. Aaron Rodgers	103.8
2. Russell Wilson	98.9
3. Tom Brady	97.3
4. Tony Romo	97.1
5. Steve Young	96.8

DREW BREES

NEW ORLEANS SAINTS ←

The New Orleans Saints started in 1967, but didn't have a winning season until 1987!

QBs are all tall, powerful players, right? Down in New Orleans, there's a quarterback who experts said was too short to be a star.

They were wrong.

Drew Brees has passed for 5,000 yards or more in a season four times. That's the most ever. He topped 4,000 yards six more times! He led the NFL in **completions** five times. He was No. 1 in touchdown passes four times. Though just about six feet tall, he has one of the biggest hearts in the game. Few QBs can match his toughness and his will to win.

Brees led the Saints to their only Super Bowl win. In Super Bowl XLIV, Brees threw 2 TD passes and was the MVP of the game. New Orleans beat the Indianapolis Colts, 31–17.

NUMBERS, NUMBERS

Drew Brees has the top three seasons all-time for completions. He also has six of the top 10!

1. 471 completions in 2016
2. 468 completions in 2011
3. 456 completions in 2014

JOHN ELWAY

DENVER BRONCOS

This strong-armed passer had a long wait for his Super Bowl ring. Elway led the Denver Broncos to three Super Bowls in the 1980s . . . but they lost all three. He had a strong arm and he was not afraid to run with the ball. Each time, though, the championship slipped away.

He kept trying. He was one of the hardest throwers and bravest QBs in the league. Like many great QBs, he was a leader. His team looked to him for inspiration time and again.

Finally, he got another chance. In 1997, at the age of 37, Elway led Denver to the Super Bowl. This time, he led them to victory! Denver won 31–24 over Green Bay. Then Elway did it again the next year! The cherry on top? He was named the Super Bowl XXXIII MVP! Now that's the way to retire!

Elway had one of the strongest throwing arms ever. If a receiver missed the ball and it hit him, the seams of the ball would leave a mark. The X of the laces was known as "The Elway Cross." Ouch!

NUMBERS, NUMBERS

Big and strong, Elway was tough to tackle. He scored 33 rushing touchdowns in his 16-year career.

BRETT FAVRE

Tough. Dependable. A leader. A winner. All those words describe Brett Favre (FARV). He played 299 games in a row at QB. No one has a longer streak. When he retired in 2010, no one had ever thrown more TD passes. No one had more passing yards.

Favre is certainly Green Bay's greatest quarterback. He led the Packers to victory in Super Bowl XXXI. It was their first in 28 seasons. Favre won three NFL **MVP awards** in a row (1995–1997).

He had a super-strong passing arm. He was never afraid to run the ball, either. Favre was tough, and played while injured. He wrapped up his amazing career with the New York Jets and Minnesota Vikings.

Favre led the Packers to the playoffs 11 times. Then he was the QB for Minnesota when they played in the 2009 postseason.

NUMBERS, NUMBERS

Career Passing Yards: 71,838—That's more than 40 miles!

All-Time Record: 10,169 pass attempts

All-Time Record: 6,300 completions

PEYTON MANNING

INDIANAPOLIS COLTS • DENVER BRONCOS

Peyton Manning probably has a really big trophy case! He is the only player with five NFL MVP awards. He earned a pair of Super Bowl rings—one each with Indianapolis and Denver. He also holds the records for most career TD passes and most passing yards. Manning was a great passer and a strong leader. Unlike many QBs, he called most of his own plays.

Manning played for the Colts from 1998–2010. He turned them from losers into Super Bowl winners. He had to miss a season with a neck injury, but came back with the Denver Broncos and won again! He set all sorts of records and led that team to Super Bowl 50. In the final game of his great career, he beat Tom Brady and the Patriots. Manning walked off the field a champion!

NUMBERS, NUMBERS

- Peyton's 49 touchdown passes in 2004 were a single-season record . . . until Tom Brady threw 50 in 2007. Then Peyton topped that with 55 in 2013!

- His 5,477 passing yards in 2013 are also an all-time best.

Peyton's dad Archie played QB in the NFL for 14 seasons. Peyton's brother Eli is the longtime QB of the New York Giants.

9

DAN MARINO

MIAMI DOLPHINS

Dolphins' receivers had to be on their toes. No QB zipped the ball out faster than Miami QB Dan Marino. Big and tall, Marino was also super-quick. He led the Dolphins for 17 seasons, setting many passing records. He was tops in the NFL in passing yards five times. In 1984, he became the first QB ever with 5,000 passing yards in a season. He had 5,084 while leading the Dolphins to the Super Bowl. He also set a single-season record with 48 TD passes. His record wasn't topped until 2007!

Marino was not a **scrambler**. He usually didn't have to run. He was able to get his passes off so quickly! In 10 seasons, he was sacked the least of any starting QB.

Marino was a fiery leader. He was never afraid to inspire his teammates to win!

NUMBERS, NUMBERS

36: That's how many times Marino led his team to victory when they trailed in the fourth quarter. It was the most ever when he retired. Only two passers have topped him since then.

The Fake Spike: Late in a game against the Jets, Marino pulled one of the best tricks ever. He pretended to spike the ball to stop the play. Then he pulled the ball up and threw a touchdown pass! Everyone on the Jets was fooled . . . and so were some fans! Miami won the game!

WARREN MOON

EDMONTON ESKIMOS (CFL)
HOUSTON OILERS • MINNESOTA VIKINGS

Only one QB has been a star in two countries! Warren Moon was one of the greatest passers in Canadian Football League history! Then he switched to the NFL and made the Pro Football Hall of Fame!

Moon played for the CFL's Edmonton Eskimos and led them to five Grey Cup titles. That's the CFL championship. He was one of the most accurate passers in that league.

In 1984, he moved to the NFL's Houston Oilers. He led them to the playoffs six times. Moon was not the tallest passer around. He was only six feet tall. But he had a huge heart and was a fierce competitor. He also had a powerful passing arm. His best season was 1990, when he led the NFL in attempts, completions, and passing yards. After leaving Houston, he starred for Minnesota and played briefly with Seattle and Kansas City.

Warren Moon was the first African-American quarterback elected to the Pro Football Hall of Fame. He has paved the way for many great black QBs in the years since.

NUMBERS, NUMBERS

No. 2? If you combine Moon's passing yards in the NFL and CFL, he would trail only Brett Favre on the all-time list.

TOM BRADY

NEW ENGLAND PATRIOTS

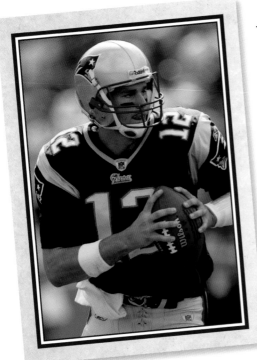

The QB with the most Super Bowl wins ever was chosen 199th in the 2000 NFL **Draft**. Tom Brady used that to inspire him to greatness.

Brady was a high school star and then played in college at Michigan. He had to wait to become a starter there. When he took over the Wolverines, he led them to a great season. He was shocked when seven other QBs were chosen before him in the draft. Then, with New England, he had to sit on the bench. Finally, in 2001, he got his chance. He led the Patriots to 11 straight wins. Then they won Super Bowl XXXVI! Brady's superstar career was on!

Brady led New England to two more Super Bowls in the next three seasons. Then in 2007, Brady and the Patriots went 16–0. They were the first undefeated team since 1972. Unfortunately, they were upset in the Super Bowl. They lost the Super Bowl again after 2011. Was Brady getting too old?

During the 2017 season, Brady set another record. He won his 200th game as a starting quarterback. That was the most ever!

To answer that question, Brady worked on his diet. He does not eat sugar and eats lots of fruits and vegetables. He works out every day, even in the offseason. That helped him stay fit when many players have retired.

First, he guided the team over Seattle in Super Bowl XLIX. Then at the age of 39, he led the Patriots to victory in Super Bowl LI. The Patriots trailed by 25 points in the fourth quarter. Brady calmly led his team on drive after drive. They tied the score and headed to **overtime**. It was the biggest comeback in NFL playoff history!

New England won in overtime! Brady became the first player with four Super Bowl MVP trophies. That's not bad for a sixth-round draft pick!

NUMBERS, NUMBERS

Brady holds these Super Bowl career records, among others:

7 Super Bowl games

15 TD passes

309 pass attempts

2,071 passing yards

OTTO GRAHAM

CLEVELAND BROWNS

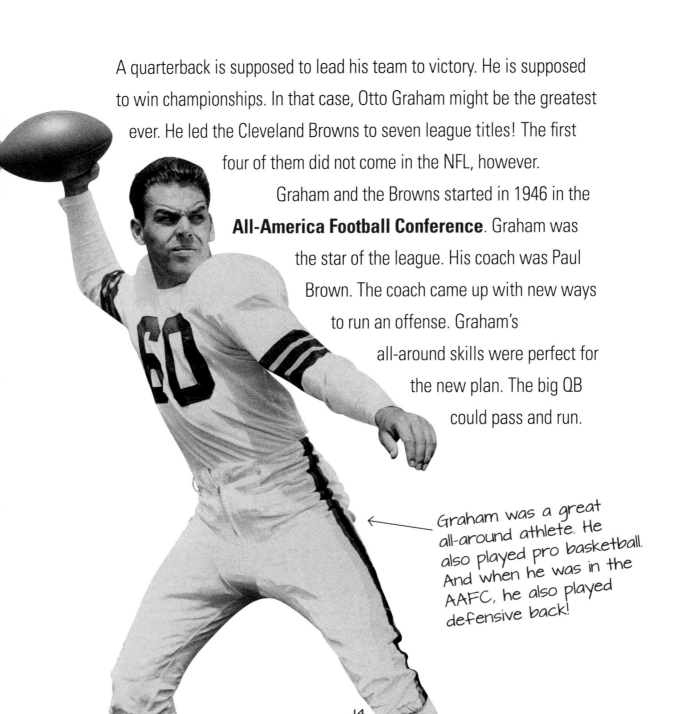

A quarterback is supposed to lead his team to victory. He is supposed to win championships. In that case, Otto Graham might be the greatest ever. He led the Cleveland Browns to seven league titles! The first four of them did not come in the NFL, however. Graham and the Browns started in 1946 in the **All-America Football Conference**. Graham was the star of the league. His coach was Paul Brown. The coach came up with new ways to run an offense. Graham's all-around skills were perfect for the new plan. The big QB could pass and run.

Graham was a great all-around athlete. He also played pro basketball. And when he was in the AAFC, he also played defensive back!

Graham and the Browns won all four championships in AAFC history. In 1950, some AAFC teams joined the NFL. Most people thought the "new" teams would not do well in the NFL. They were wrong! Graham led the Browns to the NFL championship! Graham had four TD passes as the Browns beat the Los Angeles Rams, 30–28.

Graham and the Browns repeated the feat in 1954 and 1955. In the 1954 game, Graham had three TD passes and ran for three TDs!

Cleveland also made the final game in other years. So from 1946 to 1955, Graham had his team in ten championship games. They won seven of them! That's a winner! He was elected to the Pro Football Hall of Fame in 1965.

NUMBERS, NUMBERS
- Led AAFC or NFL in passing yards five times
- Ran for 44 career TDs
- While playing defense, recovered 12 fumbles!

JOE MONTANA

SAN FRANCISCO 49ERS • KANSAS CITY CHIEFS

Montana played his final two seasons with the Kansas City Chiefs. No surprise—he led them to the AFC Championship Game!

Until Tom Brady topped him, Joe Montana was the greatest Super Bowl QB ever. He led San Francisco to four wins in the big game. In three of those Super Bowls, he was the MVP.

Montana was not the biggest QB around. He was only about six feet tall. But he had amazing football smarts. Montana just knew how to win.

He had been a college star at Notre Dame. With the 49ers, he teamed with coach Bill Walsh.

The 49ers ran a new kind of offense. It was called "West Coast." Montana was perfect for it. He could move in the **pocket**. He made good decisions, and he was very accurate. He did not lead the league in many areas. However, he was tops in completion percentage five times. He did not throw tons of TD passes. He did always seem to throw one when his team needed it most.

As a leader, Montana was always calm. One of Montana's nicknames was "Joe Cool." When things in a game were tense, he was not. In one Super Bowl, his team was driving for a winning score. The fans were screaming and his teammates were nervous. Montana looked into the stands and spotted a movie star. "Hey, guys!" he said. "Look! There's John Candy!" The 49ers all laughed! Cool and calm, Montana then led them to another Super Bowl win.

Montana was the second QB to lead his team to four Super Bowl wins. Pittsburgh's Terry Bradshaw was the first. Montana was the first with three Super Bowl MVPs. He was named to the Pro Football Hall of Fame in 2000.

NUMBERS, NUMBERS

1: That's how many times Montana had more than 13 interceptions in his 15 seasons. He was super-accurate!

JOHNNY UNITAS

BALTIMORE COLTS

Johnny Unitas is not as famous as today's QBs. For longtime fans, though, he's right at the top of the all-time list. "Johnny U" was one of the toughest guys ever to play QB. He also had a great throwing arm.

Unitas almost didn't play in the NFL. He was cut from several teams. He was playing for a **semipro** league when he got another chance with the Colts. He made the most of it.

At the time Unitas played, QBs chose all their team's plays. Unitas was a master of knowing just what play would work.

His most famous game was the 1958 NFL Championship Game. The Colts trailed late in the game. He led them down the field to set up a game-tying field goal. He had to make every pass on that drive perfectly! The game went to overtime and he drove them to the game-winning touchdown. The game made his "two-minute drill" famous. Now, every quarterback has to know how to come from behind with very little time left. He also led the Colts to the 1959 NFL championship.

NUMBERS, NUMBERS

4: Number of times Unitas led the NFL in TD passes and passing yards

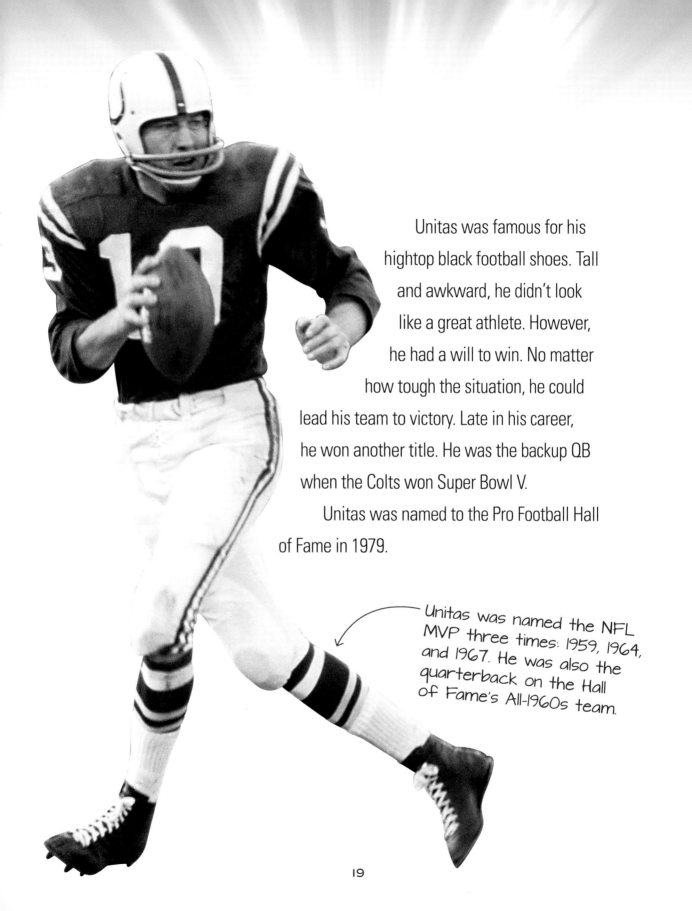

Unitas was famous for his hightop black football shoes. Tall and awkward, he didn't look like a great athlete. However, he had a will to win. No matter how tough the situation, he could lead his team to victory. Late in his career, he won another title. He was the backup QB when the Colts won Super Bowl V.

Unitas was named to the Pro Football Hall of Fame in 1979.

Unitas was named the NFL MVP three times: 1959, 1964, and 1967. He was also the quarterback on the Hall of Fame's All-1960s team.

YOUR TOP 10!

In this book, we listed our Top 10 best quarterbacks. We gave you some facts and information about each player. Now it's your turn to put the players in order. Find a pen and paper. Now make your own list! Who should be the No. 1 quarterback of all time? How about your other nine choices? Would they be the same players? Would they be in the same order as they are in this book? Are any players missing from this book? Who would you include?

Remember, there are no wrong answers. Every fan might have different choices in a different order. Every fan should be able to back up their choices, though. If you need more information, go online and learn. Or find other books about these great quarterbacks. Then discuss the choices with your friends!

THINK ABOUT THIS...

Here are some things to think about when making your own Top 10 list:

- How did each quarterback help his team win?
- What do you think a quarterback's main job is?
- Which is more important—big stats or championships?
- How does each quarterback compare with the others?
- When did he play? Has the NFL changed over time?

SPORTS GLOSSARY

All-America Football Conference (all-uh-MAYR-ik-kuh FOOT-ball KON-fur-unss)   a rival league to the NFL that played from 1946–49

completions (kum-PLEE-shuns) passes that are caught by a receiver

draft (DRAFT) the event at which NFL teams choose college players to join their teams

MVP awards (EM-VEE-PEE uh-WARDZ) honors given to players voted as the most valuable in a sports league

opinion (oh-PIN-yun) something that is believed rather than known for certain because of facts

overtime (OH-ver-tyme) time added to a sports event if it is tied after regulation time

pocket (PAH-ket) the area behind the line of scrimmage where the quarterback can throw from, created by a screen of blockers

quarterback (KWOR-ter-bak) the most important position in football; calls plays, makes passes, hands the ball off, or runs

scrambler (SKRAM-bler) a quarterback who is good at running

semipro (SEM-ee-proh) teams that use players who also have other jobs away from the field

touchdown (TUTCH-down) when the football is carried into or caught in the end zone for six points

FIND OUT MORE

IN THE LIBRARY

Savage, Jeff. *Football Super Stats*. Minneapolis, MN: Lerner Books, 2017.

Sports Illustrated Quarterbacks: The Greatest Position in Sports. New York, NY: Sports Illustrated, 2014.

Tustison, Matt. *Super Quarterbacks: 12 Great Leaders from NFL History*. Mankato, MN: 12-Story Books, 2016.

ON THE WEB

Visit our Web site for links about Top 10 quarterbacks: **childsworld.com/links**

Note to Parents, Teachers, and Librarians: We routinely verify our Web links to make sure they are safe and active sites. So encourage your readers to check them out!

INDEX

ABOUT THE AUTHOR

K. C. Kelley has written dozens of books for young readers on everything from sports to nature to history. He worked as an editor and writer with the National Football League. One Halloween when he was kid, he dressed as the ghost of Fran Tarkenton, a Hall of Fame QB (look him up!). Kelley lives with his family in Santa Barbara, California.